Pigspurt's Daughter
by Daisy Eris Campbell

Director, actor, writer, Daisy Eris Campbell grew up in the lunatic world of her father, master storyteller Ken Campbell, described by The Guardian obituary as the most original and unclassifiable talent in British theatre of the past half-century. Daisy was literally conceived backstage at her father's 12-hour staging of Robert Shea and Robert Anton Wilson's epic production of Illuminatus!, in which her mother Prunella Gee played Eris, the 50-foot Goddess of Discord. In Pigspurt's Daughter, Daisy presents a surreal and comedic monologue that magnificently continues her family legacy of lunacy.

Prior to Pigspurt's Daughter, Daisy adapted and directed Robert Anton Wilson's Cosmic Trigger in 2014 and 2017 in Liverpool and London to great acclaim. She also directed The KLF's comeback, Welcome to the Dark Ages. She worked with her father for many years on productions, notably directing the world's longest play The Warp, and a West-End run of Macbeth in Pidgin English, Makbed. Pigspurt's Daughter is her first solo show.

"Comedic, meticulously crafted genius and a joyful ride from start to finish."
— Theatre Box

"A joy to travel alongside her."
— London Theatre

"Pigspurt is a trickster, a provocateur, who incites Campbell junior to search for her real self by doing something that will surprise it into existence."
— The Reviews Hub

"The theatre needs this kind of dynasty."
— View from the Cheap Seat

"Magical, metaphysical, moving and magnificent"
— Shaun Prendergast

"This is the best. I loved it and was so inspired by it. Brilliant fascinating exquisite shit."
— Nina Conti

"Fizzing with synchronicity, Pigspurt's Daughter slices through the kipple like an expertly-wielded wooden tie, creating an ephemeral entropy embargo-cult whose sole aim is to Hail our cathartic truebadour Daisy Campbell, as she unspins her expertly-conceived fractal mind-dive. Five Pies."
— Bloke on Twitter

"The funniest, most bizarre two hours I have spent in ages. What a brilliant performance!"
— Lynda Sebire

"Pigspurt's Child is a wonderfully funny, intriguing, mesmerising and alarming show. Beautifully written and performed by Daisy Campbell, who invokes her father's eccentric, anarchic spirit in many more ways than one. A fond memoir, and a stunning comedic exorcism. Seekers: seek it!"
— Terry Johnson, playwright of Ken, Prism and Hysteria (all Hampstead Theatre Productions)

"Shouldering the visionary Campbellian tradition, Daisy Eris Campbell has become a revered figure in her own right, helping engender a nascent counterculture by heroically adapting Robert Anton Wilson's 'Cosmic Trigger' to stage in 2014 and 2017, and directing Bill Drummond and Jimmy Cauty's anarchic behemoth of a comeback, 'Welcome to the Dark Ages' in 2017. She's become a touchstone for esoteric knowledge and her work is always brimming with mind-expanding ideas."
— Liverpool Arts Lab

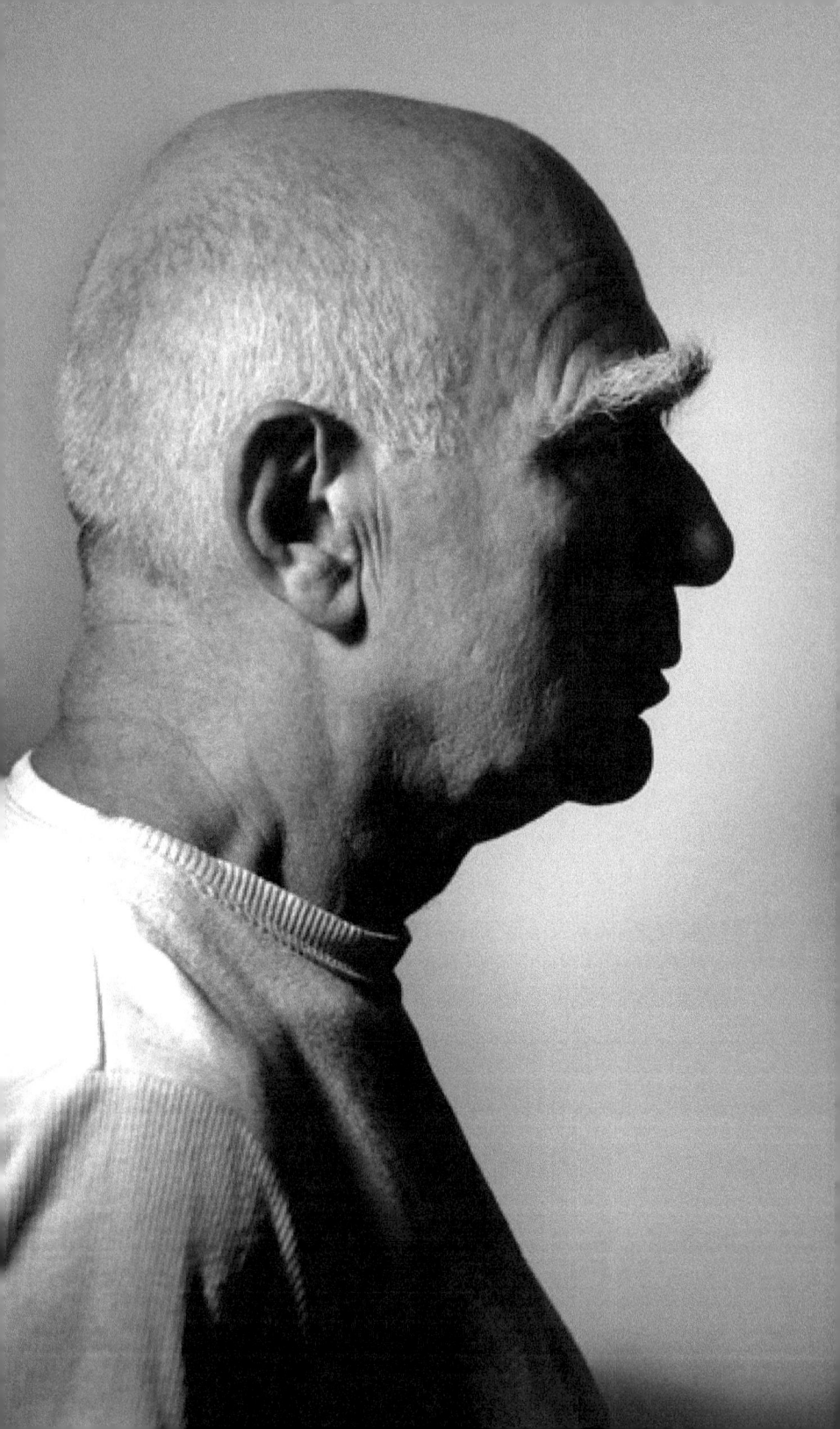

Pigspurt's Daughter

A MYTHIC DAD / A LEGACY OF LUNACY

Daisy Eris Campbell

Introduction by
John Higgs

Copyright © 2018 Daisy Eris Campbell

All rights reserved. No part of this book, in part or in whole, may be reproduced, transmitted, or utilized, in any form or by any means, electronic or mechanical, including photocopying, recording, or by any information storage and retrieval system, without permission in writing from the publisher, except for brief quotations in critical articles, books and reviews.

International Standard Book Number: 978-0-9987134-8-9

Print Edition 2020, Hilaritas Press

eBook Edition 2020, Hilaritas Press

Performance Tour: 2018

Mosbunall photos are from the personal collection of Daisy Eris Campbell. The photo of Daisy brandishing the wooden tie was taken by Lucie Blockley at the Hampstead Theatre, London. Photos from the October 6th, 2018 performance at the Cockpit Theatre in London were captured from a video made by Tim Newton.

Cover Design by Richard Rasa
eBook design by Pelorian Digital

Hilaritas Press, LLC.
P.O. Box 1153
Grand Junction, Colorado 81502
www.hilaritaspress.com

With heartfelt thanks to:

Kate Alderton (The Chariot)
Viv Boot
Claudia Boulton
David Bramwell
Claire Callender (Half of Death)
Rupert Callender (The other half of Death)
Mitch Davies
Greg Donaldson (Four of Wands)
Alistair Fruish (Art)
Prunella Gee
Andrin Hausammann (The Fool)
John Higgs (The Queen of Swords)
The Horkosians
The JAMs
Terry Johnson
Michelle Olley (The Prince of Wands)
Jonathan Rowland
Tom Schuller
Dominic Search (Five of Swords)
Jeremy Stockwell
Michelle Watson (Lust)
Dave Wybrow (Ace of Wands)
Dad

Table of Contents

Foreword by John Higgs	XIII
Pigspurt's Daughter	1
Review of Pigspurt's Daughter by Jason Watkins	95
Some Family Photos	101

FOREWORD

By John Higgs

There are two types of magical people. The first group are those who want to be magical. They feel drawn to the magical life and they read plenty of books to find out about it. They study hard and discuss arcane subjects with like-minded wizards and witches. Magic is a vocation and something to be nurtured, and they apply themselves.

The second type are people who just are magical, and there's not a damn thing that they can do about it. Their lives are a constant parade of unbelievable and impossible situations. Synchronicities compete for their attention. The world bends itself into unnatural positions, in order to better reflect their own mental landscape. Their lives are constantly, intensely magical, and they just put up with it as best they can.

The author of this play, Daisy Campbell, is this second type of person.

Her work is an unavoidable extension of this. She is a theatre director, but I sometimes suspect that she only casts her internal processes out onto the stage because it causes less trouble than casting them out into the wider world. It's a practice that works well - all the correct actors and crew turn up as needed, as if kindly provided by the universe, and she shapes and directs them in order to externalise her internal energies bubbling inside. Directing, then, provides Daisy with rare moments when she is in control of events, which is a much-needed respite from all the impossibilities that make up her normal waking hours.

Daisy is not a theatre director because she wants to provide an interesting piece of entertainment for her audience. Her interest is in transformation. She doesn't want the audience that leaves her work to be the same as the audience that walked in. This takes certain skills and techniques to achieve, and it is rare that this process can be contained within the standard parameters of theatre. The play that made her name as a director, *The Warp*, was 24-hours long. 24-hours, it goes without saying, really isn't a suitable length for a theatre performance, but sitting through it will certainly have an effect.

Or for another example, consider her stage adaptation of Robert Anton Wilson's *Cosmic Trigger*. For a brief moment this looked like it could have become a standard play, but it very quickly started to expand and mutate, and before we knew where we were, it had turned into a two-day festival that kickstarted a cultural renaissance in the British counterculture.

This was relatively sedate compared to the project which followed *Pigspurt's Daughter*, the Cerne-to-CERN pilgrimage. This involved 69 people travelling from the ancient priapic British hill figure the Cerne Abbas Giant to the CERN Large Hadron Collider in

Geneva – a journey from the large hard-on to the Large Hadron. For the pilgrims present the experience was absolutely transformative, as they found themselves gleefully being woven into a loved-up 138-legged supra-individual. That adventure is a tale for another day, but suffice to say that although that event was technically not theatre, it absolutely was theatre. Or at least, it was what theatre will become once the division between audience and performers has been removed, and once all the theatres have been burnt down.

Which is what makes *Pigspurt's Daughter* something of an oddity. It is a Daisy Campbell project that more-or-less remains within the bounds of an established theatrical tradition. That tradition is the absurdist monologue, which is the form most associated with her late father, the maverick performer Ken Campbell. This was very much the point of the exercise. *Pigspurt's Daughter* was performed 10 years after his death, during a year in which Daisy attempted to sort out the baggage, both emotional and physical, of her father's legacy. One result of this is an archive of his performances, co-produced with David Bramwell, which you can find for free if you search for 'Seeker Ken Campbell' in your podcast app.

In *Pigspurt's Daughter*, Daisy climbs inside her father's work, simultaneously resurrecting him and laying him to rest. She channelled his spirit, owned it and moved past it, giving a performance every bit as mesmerising, funny and mind-expanding as her father at his best. I think many of us, wowed as we were by the performance, hoped that it would be the start of something. The baton had been passed from father to daughter, we thought, and the world would be able to look forward to brand new Daisy Campbell absurdist monologues touring the country every year or two.

It does not look as if that is the plan. Daisy is more interested in giving us what we need, rather than what we want. She's not here to entertain us. She wants to suck us all into that extraordinary magical world that she lives in and see how we like it.

Pigspurt's Daughter is an illustration of what we could have expected if Daisy had wanted to be recognised as great, instead of wanting us to be great. A review of it won the 2019 Observer/Anthony Burgess prize for arts journalism, which shows that it was sufficiently self-contained that a critic could put a frame around it. No critic could do justice to the Cerne-to-CERN pilgrimage in 1500 words, in comparison, for a 100,000-word book would only begin the discussion. Having heard early discussions about her post-Cerne-to-CERN projects, it's safe to say that they won't be constrained by the boundaries of a standard theatre project, or indeed, by any set of rational boundaries currently existing. All this makes the record of this project that you hold in your hands a rare and special thing.

This is not to say that *Pigspurt's Daughter* is a normal play, or course. A number of innocent audience members attended the performance expecting a night of passive entertainment and found themselves in the

Swiss Alps months later grappling with the extent to which their life had been permanently changed. Nor is it true to say that it is not magical. There is an incident in the story which was invented for plot reasons, but the performing of the play immediately caused that fictional incident to come true, in circumstances that were far more improbable than in the play. *Pigspurt's Daughter* may be the one piece of Daisy's work that has been deliberately constrained by a standard theatrical form, but it is still trouble.

Of all of Daisy Campbell's work, this is the one that can best be contained within the pages of a book. Reading it, therefore, should be safe. Or at least, relatively safe. Probably. Look, you never can tell what exposure to Daisy or Daisy's work is going to bring. You just have to dive in and see.

John Higgs
Brighton, August 2019

Pigspurt's Daughter

A MYTHIC DAD / A LEGACY OF LUNACY

"It was the year they finally imminentized the eschaton" –
That, Spores, is the opening line of *Illuminatus!* –
by Robert Shea and Robert Anton Wilson –
The eschaton, that's the end of the world –
and to imminentize is to bring it on, to make it more imminent –
And I've been re-reading bits of it recently looking for clues into a recurring dream:

A brick pyramid rises from a dilapidated sooty cityscape –
strange activity –
the rattle of supermarket trollies –
banging of traffic cones –
a carnival of people with their faces grotesquely painted –
I am already dead.
I watch from above the brick shard –
These creatures are perhaps our great-great-greatgrandchildren –
One of the feral children looks up to where I hover, invisible,
and bellows *chaos never died* and a great cheer rings out –
One of the skull creatures begins to climb up the brick pyramid –

and in their hand is the final brick –
They're going to place it on the top –
But it's then that I see there's a gap –
right at the bottom –
And I'm always trying to shout from my disembodied vantagepoint –
There's a gap! –
But it's too late the top brick has been placed –
the gap will remain –
And I am just a scream in the sky.

Anyway that's my weird dream –
don't worry it's not all like that –
Hello, thanks for coming –
It's ten years since the untimely death of my father,
     Ken Campbell
described as theatre maverick, genius (in the original
     sense of the word), antic visionary –
Some of you may know his work –
but if you don't, don't worry –
Over the course of this evening you'll get some idea of
     the man.

So yes, ten years since he died –
That's why I'm doing this show –
It's why I'm spending my year sifting through his
     archive:
his notebooks, his newspaper cuttings, his weird
     letters, weird scripts, paintings made from parrot
     shit –
here's the provocatively titled 'The Bombing of
     Baghdad' –
here's a boudoir made for his nose –
his wooden tie used to fight an assailant in his first solo
     show,
The Recollections of a Furtive Nudist –
a fisherman's jacket to wear to his Hackney Marsh
     office –
which was a wooden picnic table in the heart of the
     marshes –
where he'd conduct his marsh business –
What's in here? –

His teeth in case he needed to hold an impromptu
	ventriloquism workshop –
Oh look his ping pong ball –
To train people in how to look like you're just about to
	be funny in a moment –
See? Just about to be funny in a moment –
Ah yes, his dick nose and laughing mirror –
My dad's favourite cure for the blues –

People sometimes called my dad mad –
'I'm not mad' he'd say –
'I'm not mad –
I've just read different books' –

It was on Hackney marshes by the Lee Navigational
	that we lived –
with our boat The Snark moored nearby –
the rowing club and Fred's cafe a one minute stroll
	away –
We'd go fishing for supermarket trollies in the canal at
	the weekend –
with a magnet strong enough to pick up a car –
Or make films in the vast abandoned water purifying
	beds –
After I'd have an orange by the neck at The Anchor
	and Hope pub overlooking the canal –
while dad held forth to the local gongoozlers –
When I was young and ever so sweet –
he was a brilliant dad.

When I was in my teens he got a gig for Channel 4 –

interviewing all the philosophic greats of our time –
with this question:
what or where is our Self? –
It was for a documentary called Brain-Spotting –

'Where do you see me? (he'd say)
Yes, yes, I'm on the stage –
but where do YOU see me? –
(don't worry, this is how he talked) –
In your eyes? –
Really? –
You see me with your eyes, but then that's relayed
    where? –
Inside your head – Okay – onto what? –
A screen? –
And who's watching the screen? –
Is that YOU? Is that your SELF? –
But then the chaps who get paid to ponder these things
    say:
that geezer watching the screen must have another
    little geezer inside him –
who's watching another (titchy) screen –
and there must be another geezer inside that –
and another geezer inside that –
which would be ridiculous…
And anyway, brainial surgeons can't find that bit –
They can take the top of your head off and ping a bit
    here and your left leg goes up –
Or they can pang this bit there and you're talking about
    your Granny –
But they can't find any YOU

Any SELF –
And it's a thing we need, the SELF –
A thing we think must be there –
But a thing we haven't yet found.

You've got to take stories to the end of the line –
That is my attempt to impersonate Robert McKee –
Original Hollywood Screenwriting guru –
A brusque, suave, straight-talking American –
Who does legendary three-day intensive story structure courses –
Still does them, now into his 80s.
My dad took me to a Robert McKee story structure course when I was 11 –
I spent much of the 12 hour days doodling princesses – but I loved it –
And from then on me and dad talked in story structure –
'Are you planning on an inciting incident today, Daisy? Or are you staying in bed?' –
Staying in bed, give me a shout when we're at the third act climax! –
On journeys in his little van he'd quiz me on structure jargon:
'What's a set-up?'
It's a bit of the story that seems relatively unimportant –
'What's the pay-off?'
When later it turns out that it was important –
I also did Robert McKee's horror course –
but I can only remember something about vaginas with teeth –

Probably a bit young for that one.

And so we learnt from McKee that you have to take stories to the end of the line –
To do this you have to find what he calls the Negation of the Negation –
that is, if your story is told along a certain value line –
for example, along the line of love and separation –
then you need to make your characters experience the ultimate furthest end of that line –
To cause the audience to experience something they haven't experienced before –
A whole new catharsis –
As you know – Catharsis literally means Cleansing and Purging Through Drama.
So along this line of, for example, love and separation –
we've got to show the love end –
but this has got to be a special love of some kind –
Then separation –
maybe the death of the loved one –
but what could be the end of the line with that one? –
Loss of the memories of the loved one? –
A realization that the loved one was not who you thought they were?
A realization that it is you, not the loved one who is in fact dead? –
Etc. etc. . . . you see, you're always trying to find the negation of the negation –

Dad loved this –

Poor playwright pals who'd made the mistake of inviting Ken to their opening night would be nobbled in the bar afterwards:

'Your problem, you see, is you haven't found *the negation of the negation.*'

Then McKee taught us *The Gap* –
The story happens in The Gap –
The gap is what exists between your expectation of what should reasonably happen in a reasonable universe populated by reasonable people –
and what actually happens –
So you knock on a door and the person you expect to open it is there? –
No story –
They say what you expect them to say? –
No story –
Now, you knock on a door, no-one answers –
but you find the door is unlocked and you go inside –
There's shit and feathers all over the walls, a parrot is flapping madly and there's the sounds of dogs whining from another room –
See? –
Possibility of a story –
The gap has opened –
Like what is actually there instead of a Self.

Another thing I learned about story structure (not from McKee this) –
was the difference between a character's psychological need –

and their moral need –
So their psychological need is to confront the ghost
    from their past –
or find their purpose or whatnot –
But their moral need is something they are doing,
    which is hurting other people –
and which they are not aware of –

And I used to live on a commune full of psychonauts –
which is a snazzy word for people who conduct
    experiments with psychedelics –
some of them whilst doing PhDs –
most of them not –
This was when I first became a single mum –
when my daughter was about three-
Over dinner one night I was telling them about the
    difference between a character's psychological
    need and their moral need –
and I mused –
I wonder what my moral need is? –
I wonder what I'm doing which is inadvertently
    hurting those around me? –
And they all stopped eating, and stared at me –
Clearly they knew exactly what my moral need was –
And they said:
Sort your nits out! –
Oh god the nits –

Me and my daughter had nits for years –
We gave them to all the psychonauts in the commune –
and all the psychonauts' friends –

which disturbed their psychonautical adventures –
One dreadlocked psychonaut had to dip his head in a
  bucket of diesel to get some sweet relief –
Another, sad to relate –
She had to be sectioned –
after a nit fell out of her hair whilst she was tripping
  and told her the secret of life –
To be fair the nit was probably tripping too –
But what sent her over the edge was that she couldn't
  resist the urge to squash it –
She went on to give tripping nits to the entire
  psychiatric ward –
Oh God, my moral need!

But I couldn't do it –
I was too morally bankrupt, and my daughter's nits
  were too overwhelming –
So when, a few years later –
after my daughter and I had been ejected from the
  psychonauts' commune –
for more than just nit-related crimes –
but that didn't help –
I found a woman who was guaranteeing to kill nits by
  hoovering them up with special attachments –
and her ladies wore sexy Barbarella-style white
  outfits –
emblazoned with Lice Assassin –
And before I knew it I had my own little franchise that
  I ran from my back room in Brighton, hoovering
  nits –
And I ran that franchise for about three years –

then one day, hoovering a particularly infested,
    infuriatingly ungrateful teenager –
I realised I could never look at another nit –
What must have happened was this:
I must have finally hoovered up as many lice as me
    and my daughter had originally spread –
The cosmic score was settled –
I had vanquished my moral need.

But what *really* taught me most about story was
    watching Dad's one-man shows over and over
    again –
(cheaper than a babysitter) –
Even the great man McKee reckons my dad was the
    greatest storyteller he ever met –
And Dad's performing his strange tales round and
    about –
above fetish pubs –
under occult bookshops –
And then his old mate Richard Eyre gets the gig of
    Artistic Director at the National Theatre – and
    suddenly Ken's got a National Theatre commission
    for his next show!

Richard Eyre: 'So Ken I just wanted to check in on
    how the next show is going?' –
Ken: *Oh, it's going alright –*
'Do we know what form it's going to take?' –
Yes. Not stand-up comedy –
but sit-down tragedy! –
A comic epic science fiction conspiracy weepie! –

Richard: 'You are aware that our audiences aren't as bright as the ones you're used to?' –
No?
'Oh yes, you're used to your loyal bunch who turn up in some part-converted bacon-curing works –
and they've really come to be there –
to be there with you –
A lot of ours just come –
To have been there' -
Ken: *Oh. So I should make it short?*
'Oh no! Ours like to suffer –
That's all become part of it. They expect that –
I'm just a bit worried –
You see, our last one-man show was this dangling French Canadian –
Our audience might be a bit phased if they find themselves following yours' –
So – make it obscure?
'Oh yes. Make it obscure, but not so obscure that it couldn't be cleared up in a few lines from Michael Billington'.

What Dad went on to write for the National Theatre was a solo show called *Pigspurt* –
The synopsis is as follows:
Having had it pointed out by Buster Bloodvessel –
front man of Bad Manners –
(who drank at the Anchor and Hope pub) –
that Ken's nose actually looked like the backside of a woman –
(I'm now pointing to the pic)

Look, see, there's her back, there's the crevice of the
 buttocks –
her legs are kind of out like she's sitting cross-legged –
and you can't see her hair cos she washing it –
Anyway Ken becomes obsessed with finding *the
 woman who's arse matches his nose* –

through which pursuit he accidentally invokes
    Pigspurt –
an entity he learns about from Philip K Dick.

Dad was a post-VALIS Dickhead –
VALIS: VAST ACTIVE LIVING INTELLIGENCE
    SYSTEM –
This definition of Pigspurt from the glossary to Dick's
    Exegesis –
"Pigspurt – Philip K Dick often felt that there dwelled
    within his psyche what seemed to be a second
    entirely other self –
Pigspurt: a malevolent force that had filled him with a
    craven attitude toward governmental authority –
At times Dick believed that the identity of this second
    self was the late James A Pike" –
(Incidentally, that's Bishop Pike, the heretical bishop
    of
California who came to believe that Jesus was a
    mushroom) –
But then as Dad's quest continues to find the woman
    who's arse matches his nose –
he happens to catch sight of his own arse in the
    mirror –
and realises –
It was his own arse he sought!

So to celebrate the fact that I'd killed my last nit –
I did an MSc in Transpersonal Psychology and
    Consciousness Studies –
The first thing I learnt, is that neuroscientists have been

unable to locate a Self –
Yes, Dad, I know you already knew that –
But here's the new question –
What is the thing in our brains that makes us think we have a Self? –

Enter a neuroscientist chap called Gazzaniga and his famous split-brain experiments –
He found these patients who'd had their corpus callosums –
(the bit that connects the two halves of the brain) –
their corpus callosums severed –
This was a technique used in the seventies for sufferers of particularly severe epilepsy –
and basically they functioned fairly normally, these people with split-brains –
Occasionally there'd be silliness –
one arm opening the car door –
whilst the other kept closing it –
but even the silliness didn't seem to bother them –
What Gazzaniga found was that if he stuck you split-brain patients in front of a screen and flashed two words at you –
one on either side of the screen –
an odd thing happens –
You literally cannot see the word on the left –
So if I ask you to draw the word obviously you won't be able to –
But if I ask you to draw the first thing that comes to your mind –
you will draw the word you couldn't see –

19

But this is the thing! –
If I ask you why you drew that particular thing, you'll start making stuff up –
If you'd seen the word bell –
you'll be telling me about how you'd heard the church bells ringing on your way in –
If you've drawn an oven –
you're flapping that you've left the oven on –
In other words, you'll say anything that seems vaguely plausible –
Any bollocks –
and not only that –
YOU'LL BELIEVE IT!
Even if I tell you that the word bell was on the screen –
you'll still maintain that be that as it may –
the reason you drew it was because the church bells were so uplifting –
and your aunt was a campanologist –
blah blah blah –
Gazzaniga called this brain-function The Interpretor –
Another chap named it The Narrator –
or my favourite –
The Storyteller –
And it's the Storyteller that masquerades as the Self.

It's a thing we need, the SELF
A thing we think must be there –
But a thing we haven't yet found –
Yeah you're right, Dad –
They haven't found the Self –
But they've found the geezer who masquerades as it –

So this Storyteller geezer located somewhere in my left hemisphere just pumps out the illusion of a self, does it? –
Pumps out the illusion of purpose and meaning? –
This seemed distinctly fishy to me –
I grew increasingly suspicious of The Storyteller –
I tried ignoring it but it rattled on regardless –
I began to imagine what wonders might lurk in the totality of me –
if they didn't first have to pass through the wretched Storyteller.
I began to fantasize about snuffing it out altogether –
The Storyteller –
With its parochial worldview –
its soap-opera sensibilities –
knitting away its coherent, sensible narrative –
narrowing my life-story into yet another tale of *and then I did this, and then I did that . . .*

No! Not for me! –
I did The Robert McKee's Story Structure Course when I was 11! –
If it was a storyteller I was going into battle with, then I was equipped –
I was going to force open a Gap –
between what The Storyteller expected to happen in my reasonable life populated with reasonable people –
and what was actually going to happen –
And that's where things started to get interesting –
I discovered that if you feed it set-ups, you can keep it

whirring away –
desperately trying to find the *pay-off* –
For example, I began to distribute a pack of Aleister Crowley tarot cards –
I'd sidle up to folk who seemed to be on some kind of important mission, and conspiratorially offer them a tarot card –
No - keep it, I'd say. You're now the keeper of that card until
further notice –
That's a nice little set-up –
Storyteller! How you gonna pay that off? –
Will I call them all in, the keepers of the cards, for some secret mission? Some theatrical illuminati? –
And I tell you, once you start mucking with your Storyteller, weird shit happens –
Bizarre synchronicities occur –
freaks come out of the woodwork bearing clues –
dreams become technicolour –
Storyteller! Why did I just meet that person? –
Storyteller! Why did I just read that book? –
Storyteller! What is the recurring dream about the gap in the brick pyramid? –
Storyteller whizzing desperately to keep up -
Manufacture meaning! –
Find a coherent story! –

But then I started to feel rather dicky –
I'd over-fed my Storyteller with too many set-ups –
And there were no pay-offs in sight! –
The glorious meaning that The Storyteller had

manufactured began to crumble . . .

The last time I'd felt this mad I'd ended up in a Loony Bin somewhere in Kent.

I'd been 23 and I'd just read *Illuminatus!* for the first time –
Signs and meanings were everywhere –
and I was in this place in Kent with rainbow knickers on my head, for important cosmic reasons –
I was in fact attempting to regulate the flow of cosmic pronoid synchronicities that I was experiencing –
Pronoia? - the creeping sensation that everyone, everywhere is out to help you? –
I believe paranoids favour tinfoil –
but I was pronoid, so rainbow knickers seemed more apt –
I was holding forth one day –
In my knickers –
I was telling everyone about my dad's notions about the Orificular Answer to Audience Restlessness.
Do you know this? –
Up on stage, the actors are all right because they get to move about –
But in the audience you're kind of stuck there –
After 20 minutes or so, your orifices start to concrete up a bit –
Up on stage, we can release some of the tension by subtly stressing one orifice after another –
For example, my dad saw Sir Ian McKellan –
whilst delivering a speech –

back up against the table in the interests of relieving
audience tension –
Ballet for instance, would be boring if it weren't for
the constant tension gained by the audience's
subconscious concern that the male dancers are
going to clout their bollocks on something –
And you may think, well that's hardly orificular is it? –
And you'd be right! –
It's protuberential –
The subliminal rhythm of all successful theatre is
Protuberance/Orifice –
The Protuberential/the Orificular –
A Demanding Protuberance / A Protesting Orifice –
Or in Comedy: A Wilting Protuberance / A Snapping
Orifice –

And there's this surly guy stood back from the rest of
the group –
He looks me straight in the eye and says:
*How long have you been stuck up your father's
arsehole?* –
Ooof –

I'd taken to reading everyone's fortunes from a David
Bowie tape insert –
word had got round that they were rather on the
money –
And Surly Guy turns up as if against his own better
judgment –
He says, 'go on, then' –
I look down at the song lyrics from The Bowie

Collection cassette tape insert –
It's one of those fold-out things with the tiny writing –
and it was like all the words blurred –
except one verse that looked as if it had been
    highlighted –
I remember thinking - no don't read that –
but I'd seen that he'd seen that I'd seen –
So I just read it:

All your vilest nightmares
Will Consume your shrunken head
And the ho-ho-hounds of paranoia
Will Dance upon your stinking bed

And he just looked at me and said –
'I fucking knew it'.

So back to my present dilemma –
I'd mucked with my Storyteller –
meaninglessness had descended –
I was exhausted, and not well –
I'd got this horrible fungal toe which my hippie mates
    were telling me meant my gut was out of whack –
So I managed to get along to this nutritionist woman
    who explained I had mycotoxins, this kind of
    fungus overgrowth due to too much acidity in my
    gut –
She explained that this fungi actually had an important
    job –
Its job was to eat me after my death –
But so crap had been my diet and lifestyle and whatnot
    that they'd got underway with this task already –

That really ought to have been wake-up call enough –
but I couldn't get to grips with anything –
Not even attempting to vanquish the fungi that was
    prematurely eating my corpse –

Then my great friend Kate (keeper of The Chariot
    card) told me that she'd had a dream –
(*Big News!* You don't mess about with Kate's
    dreams) –
She had dreamt I was attending some kind of
    workshop –
and the words *Big Mind* hovered above in light –
We spent some time trying to work out the
    subconscious meaning of this –
until I just googled 'big mind workshop' –
Yep, it's a thing –
and it was booking up for a fortnight hence in Paris.

Have you heard of this technique? –

It's rather brilliant actually –

It was developed by an American Zen Priest called Genpo Roshi as a way of using the West's familiarity with psychology to access high Zen meditative states –

So you talk to all these different voices that reside within you –

and the theory is that if they all get a chance to say their bit –

they won't block the possibility of you talking to your most cosmic self.

So I find myself in Paris in a class of 50 or so people –

and the way it works is this:

Genpo will ask to speak to a particular voice–

Some aspect of ourselves –

and our job is not be a smart-arse –

(he may ask to speak to that part of us later) –

no, it's to be kind of obvious –

And we have to speak from the point of view of each of these voices –

if we want to refer to the entity normally known as Daisy then we refer to a third person Self.

So he speaks first to the gatekeeper –

whose job it is to grant entry or not to inquisitive Zen Priests –

and after some discussion, we agree yes alright –

he can move on and talk to our other voices –

Then he asks to speak to the skeptic -

And we have to shift slightly in our chairs when he moves to a new voice –

'Who am I speaking to?' –
We say - The skeptic –
'What's your job?' –
To be skeptical –
'Why is that?' –
And we say things like:
so Daisy doesn't go about believing all this mumbo
    jumbo she seems to get caught up in –
Genpo says, 'so you're protecting the Self?' –
And we say yeah –
'What do you think about this workshop?' –
Well I'm very skeptical –
'What else are you skeptical about?' –
And we start throwing out things we're skeptical
    about –
then we realise it's everything! –
We're skeptical about EVERYTHING –
'Are you even skeptical about skepticism itself?' –
Yes! –

And I'm thinking of what my dad used to say to me –
Now, listen Daisy –
Don't believe in anything –
Nothing which is the product of the human mind is a
    fitting subject for belief –
but you can suppose everything –
and in fact you should –
supposing as much as poss is mind opening mind
    widening –
suppose fairies –
suppose flying saucers –

suppose in life after death –
I suppose you could suppose that one of the big
    religions had got it right to the last nut and bolt –
But listen Daisy –
Don't believe it.

So after hanging out with the skeptic for a while
    Genpo asks us to shift our positions a bit and then
    says:
'I'd like to speak to the damaged self –
Who am I speaking to?' –
The damaged self –
'What's your function?' –
To be damaged –
'That's right –
And will you ever not be damaged?'–
No –
'And what does the Self try to do to you?' –
Tries to annihilate me –
'But what value to you offer to the Self?' –
I hold *all* the damage –

And I'm thinking of all my visits to see Dad –
walking the dogs in Epping forest –
Done anything of note? –
That's what Dad would say to me when we met –
Done anything of note? –
When I told him I was having my second baby, he
    said:
'Oh no what are you going to do now? –
Oh Christ, you'll have to become a novelist' –

Done anything of note?
I'd started running workshops for the creatively stuck –
'Well', he said, unhooking the dogs from their ropes –
(the dogs always needed a lot of ropes) –
'For the first time ever, your life looks almost possible' –
Done anything of note?
I'd written and directed a short play about reincarnation –
I began to tell him about it –
'Anyway', he said, interrupting –
'Have you seen *The Wire?*'

Genpo's voice rings out and I'm back in Paris –
'I'd like to speak to the voice of The Seeker' –
The seeker! –
That's what my dad used to call his audience –
Now listen, Seekers! –

And if I was honest with myself that's what I was really doing in Paris –
I was *seeking* –
good material for my storyteller –
material to feed *my set-up addiction* –
But what of the pay-offs? –
Shouldn't I really be seeking the pay-offs now?

Back home I had muttered to a few people about doing something with my dad's work –
Maybe writing a show called *Pigspurt's Daughter?* –

And they'd looked concerned –
and said perhaps it's time to do your own thing –
separate from your dad –
And I remembered, oh yes, that's right –
I'm supposed to be getting out of his arsehole –

But I thought that I should at least get all my dad's
    archive stuff into a storage unit –
There's tonnes of this stuff –
It's been gumming up all our cupboards, the loft, under
    everyone's beds, tucked into every corner –
and it was time to get it all in one place –
So I've been stacking it up on these Screwfix shelves –
an absolute bargain at 19.99 each –
and these storage unit things are bloody expensive so
    you really have to stack the stuff up as high as you
    can –
Anyway I'd done that –
and then finally it was the day to go and start actually
    sorting it out –
And I had a new resolve as I made my way through the
    corridors of people's crap –
But when I un-padlocked the door –
Holy shit! –
Those cheap Screwfix shelves had all collapsed under
    the weight of my dead father's prodigious output –
They'd crashed over, completely blocking the door –
Shit! I could see all his papers all scrunched and
    screwed up –
And I just wept in the corridor of the storage unit –
I wept for Dad's work –

And Dad –
And the fucking Screwfix shelves –

I thought, no sod it –
I'm going to get into this unit if it kills me –
And there was a cardboard box jammed in-between the
    two collapsed shelves that crossed the door –
You have to picture it –
they hadn't just toppled into each other –
they had buckled –
and this cardboard box was right at the intersection
    point –
I thought if I could shove through whatever was in the
    box,
then I might just be able to squeeze through . . .
But when I pulled open the box –
inside was *my dad's flesh-coloured fat suit –*
I tried to get it out of the box but it was totally stuck –
so there was only one way in –

through the fat suit.

mnmmmhmmhhnn – and I'm in!

And Genpo Roshi's voice rings out –
'I'd like to speak to the Vulnerable Child –
'Who am I speaking to?' –
The Vulnerable Child –
'Just take a moment to feel what it's like to be you –
What does it feel like?' –
I feel innocent –
Impressionable –
Genpo says, 'would you say that you are the essence of
    the Self? –
There is something very pure about you isn't there?' –

And there I am in the collapsed storage unit –
surrounded by a lifetime's work –
My dad's work –

And that, Dad, was when I found *the fairy brain* –
You'd bought me a little second-hand caravan for my
    30th birthday –
It had arrived at your place in Epping –
And me and the family came round to take it on its
    maiden voyage –
We stood around the caravan –
you smoking a cigar –
and I commented that we were like a Mike Leigh
    movie –
and you said yes –
Yes, we are –

Then me and the family went off to a local campsite in
    Essex in the little caravan –
We'd wanted you to come –
but you had an audition for something –
You'd have loved it –
it was like a low-rent Butlins –
all push-pineapple-shake-a-tree –
and cheeky grubby Essex kids –

You phoned that night and I almost didn't take it –
I screened your calls a lot, because so often they
    degenerated into you telling me what a failure you
    thought I was –
But for some reason I took this one and you were so
    happy –
The audition had been a complete hoot –
You'd had them in fits –
One woman snorted up her tea –
It was for some kid's TV show –
And you loved hearing about the campsite and push-
    pinapple and grubby kids –
We chatted merrily for ages –
I remember thinking I'd take your calls more often if
    they were always like this –

The next morning, I woke up with red spots all over
    my face –
Big dark red spots –
We went for a walk in Epping Forest before we left for
    yours –
and my daughter stumbled upon what she called a fairy
    brain –

a weird looking mushroom with strange striations –
we picked it carefully and asked an old boy at the
    campsite if he knew what it was –
'Wow - that's a morel that is' –
Morels are very rare in the UK –
Highly prized mushroom, the morel' –
My daughter put her fairy brain to bed in a matchbox
    and said she would give it Grandpa –
because Grandpa likes fairy brains –
On the drive back to yours I kept pulling down the
    mirror to check my face –
Big dark red pustules all over my face –
From nowhere –

Then we got back to yours –
I knocked on the door but no-one answered –
But the door was open so I went inside –
The parrot was flapping madly around the room –
There was the sound of the dogs whimpering from the
    next door room –
It was the dogs I saw first –
all curled up and anxious –
Then I realised they were curled up around you –
I edged closer –
and saw your arm –
big blue spots all over your arm –
I raced out –
told the kids to wait in the car –
then I got low –
I lay flat on the ground, belly down and phoned mum –
Then 999 –

I wanted to go and look at you –
but I didn't dare –
So I waited in the other room and left the dogs and the
 parrot to sit with you and wait for the paramedics –
Who smile inappropriately when they arrive, because
 there's nothing they can do –
You're long dead –
The red spots have completely disappeared.

(I burn a Twenty Pound Note)

Did you know in Lithuania mushrooms are thought to
 be gifts from the dead to the poor? –
Did you know that Mycelium – the branching thread-
 like root system of mushrooms – pre-dates any
 other vegetation on this planet by over 300 million
 years? –
Did you know that mycelium forms the largest
 organism currently living on the planet? –
That we share over half our DNA with fungi? –
I was told this by a woman compelled to share her
 mycelic vision with me –
after I'd slipped her The High Priestess card –
The vision was this:
that this Mother Earth that people refer to –
it's not just the Earth in general –
it has a much more specific and ancient meaning –
The Mother is the mycelium –
and it's sentient –
I said I didn't know about that –
But I thought mycelium was a great metaphor for
 underground culture –

These tiny underground threads have to cross
    over before the critical mass is there to form a
    mushroom –
And all these brilliant outsider artists and activists and
    psychonauts and freaks are unseen by the world
    above –
but there they are, forging their threads –
and when enough of them cross over –
inevitably a cultural mushroom will appear –
The world above can see the mushroom –
but it can't see the culture beneath the ground, the
    endlessly criss-crossing threads.

We bury dad in a woodland burial park in Epping
    Forest –
His grave is marked by a wooden square with the
    silhouette of his profile cut from it –
Like a missing piece of a jigsaw puzzle –
At the bottom is a line from *Pigspurt*:
'There is something I must do'

Back in the collapsed storage unit –
I come across one of Dad's more recent projects –
The History of Comedy: Part one: Ventriloquism –
And in it he talks about how his recent Athlete's Foot
    of the arse has made him walk funny and may
    have opened up his gastromantical abilities –
What the hell is Gastromancy? –
Then I discover this:
'Gastromancers sense out spirits rectally –
when they come in they sweep the place around with

their hindquarters –
Gastromantical thinking being that spirits dwell below –
and the gastromancer's objective is to hoover up the unquiet –
which will then speak through the wall of his stomach' –
Then I hit the jackpot:
An excerpt from Circa 1860 attributed to Henry Mayhew:
(here an old Gastromancer from Peckham reveals the secrets of his trade) –
'The whole enterprise is your BUMBO –
These are your CAKES –
Between your CAKES is the BINKY –
In the BINKY is the TUSH or PATOOTIE –
(sometimes called the GRUMPER) –
and it is the GRUMPER that does the dowsing –
The tricksy bit of UP-LOADING (the spirit, demon or departed) –
is done by BACK-DOOR TRUMPET INHALE –
CHUFF OR CACK-PIPE UP-SUCTION (not the easiest thing) –
and once you got her up and in it's BUNCH TIGHT your BAMSIE STRINGS and keep her moving right up the LOON-PIPE well clear of the LABONZA –
keep her sweet and bye and bye she'll talk –
but keep her sweet mind –
cos a NARKY SPRITE'll prompt a BEEF-TEA BLOWBACK'.

I know I'm supposed to getting out of my father's
  arsehole –
But the truth is I love it in here.

So imagine my utter amazement when Genpo Roshi
  asks to speak to the next voice –
'This one is a little controversial but recent personal
  events have caused me to realise that its inclusion
  is very important –
I'd like to speak to the voice of the Asshole –
Who am I speaking to?' –
The Arsehole –
'What is your job?' –
My job is to be a complete and utter Arsehole –

And I started to feel a strange sensation in my
  BUMBO –
The GRUMPER is definitely picking something up –
I can feel that an UP-LOADING was imminent –
You're not supposed to stand up at these things, but
  it was as if something was forcing me up off my
  chair –
I tried to stay seated –
I was trying to fight it.
Genpo saw my discomfort and reassured me –
'There can be some powerful energy trapped in you,
  can't there?' –
Powerful energy alright –
I knew what was coming –
I'd read the gastromancer's instructions –
the BACK-DOOR TRUMPET INHALE –

or CACK PIPE UP-SUCTION –
OH CHRIST HERE IT COMES –
AND IT WAS IN –
AND HEADING STRAIGHT UP THE LOOM PIPE –

Genpo asks – 'Who are you?' –
I'm Pigspurt! –
'And what is your role?' –
I've come from below! –
From the mystery threads of the Great Mother –
The High Priestess, she nearly got there –
She sussed that the network of mycelium is sentient! –
that THE MUSHROOMS ARE NOT WHAT THEY SEEM! –
But she didn't make that last leap –
Oh come on Daisy, think! –
Where do you think the consciousness of the dead resides? –
It's in the mycelium!
It is the VAST ACTIVE LIVING INTELLIGENCE SYSTEM that Philip K Dick was on about –
And he's down here too –
And even that kid you killed with your David Bowie reading –
We're all here! –
And now you know how to suck us through into your world –
The clues were there all along, Daisy –
what with your fungal toe and your corpse-eating mycotoxins –
and my Athlete's Foot of the arse!

Genpo says (looking rather shaken) 'And what is your role?' –
I've come to take over Daisy's Storyteller! –
Come on now, enough of the set-ups, it's time for some payoffs –
To the end of the line, girl! –
I said - wait a minute –
Do you mean that FINALLY –
you're stuck up *my* arsehole? –
There's was a burst of maniacal laughter –
and then Oh God –
Oh no –
I was on the brink of a Beef-Tea blowback –

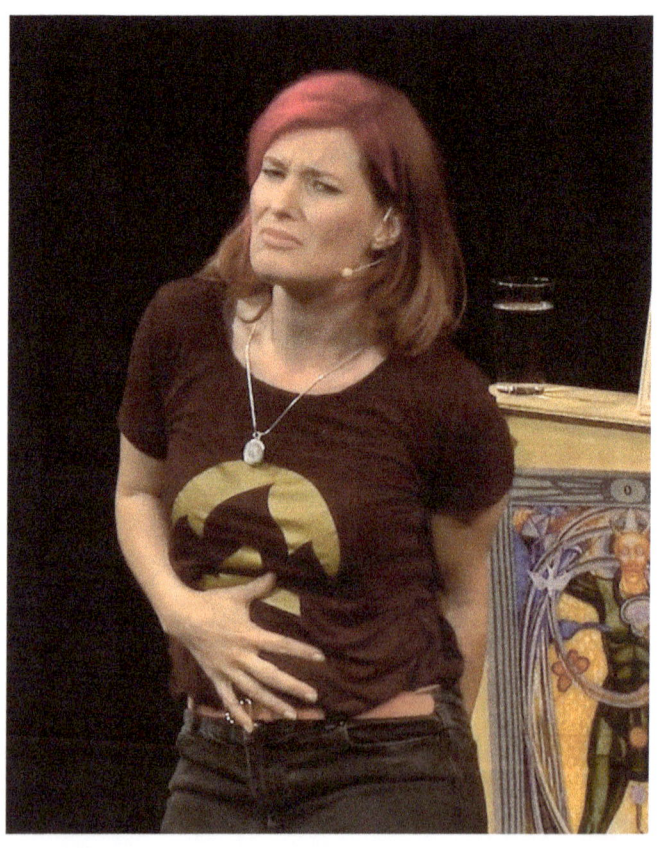

Well that seems like a good point to have an interval.

Dad did *Pigspurt* at the National Theatre and it
   won the Evening Standard Critic's Choice Best
   Comedy award –
Critics, Dad noted, never tell the truth –
At least not the whole truth, namely that in actual fact
   it's all bollocks –
There's bollocks in blank verse, bollocks with pauses –
Bollocks, Prince of Denmark, Waiting for Bollocks –
There's dreary old Russian Bollocks –
There's Brechtian bollocks –
bollocks to alienate you –
Mother Courage and her Bollocks –
Bollocks on a hot tin roof –
And critics are people who are paid to go out and
   grade the bollocks –
They can't just go out to the RSC's latest offering and
   write 'Bollocks in Tights' –
They've got to grade it –
And they graded *Pigspurt* as 'funny bollocks' and gave
   it best comedy award –

At the opening of *Pigspurt*, Ken recounts the day his
   primary school teacher Mrs O'Halloran tackled the
   subject of GOD –

Apparently we are all born with a bit of the Almighty
   in us -
we've all got our own bit of God –
and it's situated somewhere in the stomach region –
And every time you do something a bit naughty –
like tell a lie

(apparently writing a lie is even worse) –
you get a little bit of *dirty in your God.*

Every morning six year old Ken had to write up his
    diary with the rest of the class –
and if anything a wee bit sensational had happened to
    you –
maybe you'll have the honour of reading out your
    diary to the class –
And Dad used to like to go for that honour –
But very often it meant *lying in his diary.*

He wrote a little poem at that time which went:

My diary is a liary
A diary of lies
My God-All-Dirty diary
In heaven for me no pies

And throughout his life if he repeated over and over
    again:
'No pies . . . no pies . . . There's going to be no pies for
    you, Kenneth'.
The tears would stream down his face.

So, to re-cap:
There's a gap where a Self should be –
but it's filled with a Storyteller masquerading as a
    Self –
but now my dead dad is masquerading as the
    Storyteller that's masquerading as the Self –
and I summoned him in –

from the sentient mycelium below –
using an ancient rectal invocation method known as
gastromancy.

OK – is everybody with us?

He loved a good goad did my dad –
He lived to goad people to do the impossible –
His last big theatrical caper was with a bunch of actors
who called themselves the School of Night –
and could improvise ridiculous things –
like a whole new Shakespeare play –
or a Chaucerian epic –
or write sonnets as they counted backwards from 500
to 1 – in sevens! –
The improvising actors were known as the Rhapsodes,
and my dad was the Goader –
He summed his role up thus:
'I will give you impossible things to do –
then shout at you when you can't do them' –
Which also summed up his approach to parenting.

So I'm in the dimly lit collapsed storage unit –
having passed through the fat-suit –
(which is actually still stinking out my car –
as I can't quite get round to taking it to the dump –
and the dogs keep attacking it –
it's a right old crumbling mess) –
Anyway I'm sorting through all dad's stuff – this
whole
lifetime's work –

When suddenly it hits me -
This stuff is mine –
I've inherited all his stories.

That's right, says a voice from my stomach –
It's Pigspurt –
You can even tell them as if they're yours if you like –
No, I say. That wouldn't be right –
*Yeah, tell em, tell em! You say you want to do some
    kind of show to honour me –*
then you can have the lot –
if you'll do one thing for me?' –
What? –
Take it to the end of the line –
The negation of the negation –
Do we have a deal?
Tell all these stories as if they're mine . . . ? –
Ok! –
We have a deal! –

Looking around now for stories I might pinch –
There's multiple box files full of dad's research:
TV and its effects on the endocrine system of rats –
French underwater nuclear testing in the South
    Pacific –
Pidgin English translations of Shakespeare –
And the Cathars.

Dad would take me out of school for various capers
    quite regularly –
and the most memorable trip was when I was 15 –

This one was a whole tour which included:
A visit to the site in the Swiss Alps where 23 cult-
    members had burnt themselves to death in a bid
    for willful reincarnation –
A trip to Reine le Chateau, where the Holy Grail
    was thought to have rested until unearthed by an
    unscrupulous vicar in the 1800s –
who then became grotesquely vulgar –
and obscenely wealthy –
Then off to Italy to see a temple twice the size of St
    Pauls built under the ground –
And finally to Montsegor –
where the last of the Cathars were burnt at the stake in
    the 13th century by The Inquisition –
Even my jaded 16-year-old self was quite impressed
    by this trip.

Chateau de Montsegur is a vast ruined fortress atop a
    great jutting mountain –
We stayed the night in a tumble-down garret nestled
    into the mountain –
Sat in the turret window watching a storm lash the last
    stronghold of the Cathars –
I could almost see them making their final journey
    down onto The Inquisition pyres –
and leaping into the flames voluntarily –
Then laughing at their tormentors even as they burned.

The Cathars, then, along with the Discordians are the
    two family religions –
The Discordians (that's a whole other show) worship
    Chaos –

and the Cathars worship nothing –
The word Cathar comes from the same route as
 Catharsis –
the Cathars were the cleansed and purified ones –

There's been a recent outbreak of Catharism –
It's taken the form of money burning.

You can buy books on Cathars, but they don't
 REALLY tell you –
There used to be books that REALLY told you, but
 they've all been burned –
There used to be people that could REALLY tell you,
 but they've all been burned –
You date Catharism by when you got rid of it –
Eradicated 1244 –
with the fall of Montsegur –
It began acres before Jesus under other names –
Cathars believed that you shouldn't believe –
They were Gnostics, and Gnostics only gnow what
 they gnow –

and one thing that was perfectly obvious was that the
 creator is a mad barmy evil deranged demiurge –
and all matter is evil down to the last atom and quark
 of the stuff –

But what of laughter and happiness? –
That, say the Cathars, is a benign immateriality
 piercing in from the True God Almighty: The
 Nothing –
And this is not The Nothing Which Does Exist –

We speak here of The Nothing That Doth not Exist –
The Gnothing –
Also known as the Archon Domain of Eternal
    Incredible Laughter –
So not for them cold churches and vicars –
but firesides and dancing and comedians –
and although they believed that you shouldn't
    believe –
they supposed that you could suppose –
to the hilt –
to the end of the line –
end station: mass hysteria.

And I'm thinking of my dad's late pal Eddie Davies –
He gave his profession as: Eccentric Dancer, and
    Hokum Maniac –
Ed wasn't the sort of artiste to whom the likes of
    Richard Eyre could have said –
'Now, now, Edward, I think the author only intended
    titters here' . . .
Ed was a hunter of the WILD GUFFAW –
and once he had one in his sights –
he needed hysteria –
an audience helpless –
begging for LESS –
Like some of those old timers, Ed had the knack of
    suddenly so excruciating his body, that some
    audience members (particularly the older ones)
    would literally pee themselves –

In the thirties Eddie had toured in the comedy-thriller,

'Poison Piano' –
He played Toes Petersen, the deaf-mute armless
    amputee who plays the piano with his feet –
And in the third act climax when Toes learns that:
the poison is in the trousers! –
Ed's portrayal of the hapless, armless Toes, trying to
    divest his wobbly legs of the plague-soiled pants –
up the walls –
on the piano –
And in Cardiff he'd hit it –
He'd hit the Hokum High –
Clanged the Lost Chord of Comedy –
And the Cardiff audience was laughing –
weeping –
groaning –
shrieking –
choking –
farting –
pooing –
weeing –
folding –
And some Welshmen actually exploding and expiring
    in their own juices and wastes –
'How did you do that?' Ken had asked him –
'I wouldn't tell you if I knew', Eddie said –
'You don't realise the awesome power of comedy,
    Ken –
It can kill' –
'How do you feel about it now?', asked Ken –
'Any regrets?' –
Eddie thought –

and then he said –
'I just comfort myself that it was Welshmen'.

And according to dad that's what the Cathars were up
    to –
They were attempting to wind up the whole evil
    material plane –
through comedy –
Audience member: 'But aren't you talking about
    Troubadours and Minstrels and wotnot? –
and didn't they sing awful tragic mournful stuff? –
Not comedy –
That's what I was taught' –
Yes, you probably were –
but that's cos them that taught you taught you wrong –
It'd be like being four hours with Ken Dodd –
God rest his soul –
and then reporting he sang Tears For Souvenirs –
The Inquisition won! –
You were taught by the descendants of The
    Inquisition! –
The first job of the seeker on leaving school is to
    Unlearn –
Otherwise you'll never gnow gnothing.

Back in the collapsed storage unit with Pigspurt –
You see, Daisy –
all this about a missing Self –
is really just chat about the seating arrangement –
We've got the seat for a self –
but no-one sitting in it –

To get a SELF you have to ASTOUND it into being –

Wow!! –

So how you going to astound yourself a SELF, hey Daisy? –
He uses my arm to pick a book up off the floor –
Jodorowsky's Manual of PsychoMagic –
Oh yeah! (says Pigspurt) *This might help –*
Name your issue, and Jodorowsky has cooked up a potty caper that will help you fix it –

A daughter with an overbearing father! –
Oh yeah I'm sure he'll have that –
yep got it –
"The consultant should dress as a man" –
with very erotic undergarments –
then rip them up whilst screaming:
"Look at me! –
Look at me exactly as I am!
I am not an unsuccessful man!
I am a woman!" –
Hmm, says Pigspurt –
Sounds a bit squawky, that one –
Oh look -
what about some Poetic Terrorism? –
Here we go –
TAZ –
Hakim Bey –
"Walk into a city bank, take a shit and leave" –
Believe it or not, I say, I actually did that one –

Phooar, says Pigspurt. *You got up to all sorts you never told me about –*
That's cos you were too busy telling me about The Wire –
He's not listening –

Look says Pigspurt –
What's this? –
Daddy's Dreams! –
You haven't done any of these –
How's that honouring your dad? –
Haven't even ticked off a single one of his dreams –

Oh God! –
Daddy's Dreams! –
I remember that awful list –
All the things Dad longed for me to be, and would mournfully remind me about –

Give me that, I said –
Oh for fuck's sake – these are ridiculous –
Russian Gymnast –
Chinese violinist –
Those two can fuck off for starters –
Punch and Judy Professor? –
Yes, I tried that, don't you remember? –
That was the first term when I joined The Tilly Matthews Academy of Bizarre and Adventurous Education, of which you were the only teacher and I was the only pupil –
Turns out I've got the wrong shaped palette for swazzling -

Hypnotist –
I kind of did that one –
I was Miss Eris the Trance Inducer when you restaged
    The world's longest play, The Warp –
You'd send actors to me with prescriptions like 'Better
    Line Learning' –
'More Fearless' –
and I'd jsush them up with techniques I'd learned on
    that Paul McKenna weekend –
Notice the changing focus of your eyes, all that stuff –
Dog Sled racing in Anchorage? –
I suppose I could do that at some point –

Book your ticket now! –
Fuck off –
Oversee a breakthrough at CERN? –
What as in the large Hadron collider in Geneva? –
They all grin in CERN, says Pigspurt –
Well, it's not likely to happen, given I'm not an
    astrophysicist is it? –

Then the phone rang.

It was Bill Drummond from the Justified Ancients of
    Mu Mu –
Previously 90s dance group The KLF –
Bill wanted to know if I'd come and meet with him
    and his partner in crime Jimmy Cauty –

Bloody hell, said Pigspurt –
*Those are the only chaps I know who might have
    actually astounded themselves Selves –*

You're in the flow girl –
We may yet get you to the end of the line –

(Now playing a bit of 'Justified and Ancient' by The KLF –
If you're reading this, look it up on YouTube) –

Remember this? You younger ones won't –
but anyone over 40 will almost certainly know this track –
It was by the KLF. In the early 90s they were pop gods –
They were the biggest selling singles artists in the world in 1991 –
The Times recently called the second best band ever after The Beatles –
and yet many of you have never heard of them –
How did they manage that? –
Well, when they failed to have a Christmas Number One with that track that I just played –
(it had been at number one for weeks, but just before Christmas Freddy Mercury went and died) –
And this failure to have a Christmas Number One was clearly a sign that the music industry had won –
So they deleted their entire musical back catalogue –
Got the band *Extreme Noise Terror* – which does exactly what it says on the tin –
to play their number one hit at the Brit Awards in which they had just won best band –
while they stood either side of the stage and shot the audience with blanks from machine guns –

They then left a dead sheep on the steps –
Went off to bury the award statue at Stonehenge –
As the tannoy at The Brits declared:
"The KLF have now left the music industry" –

There then remained the question of what to do with
    all the money they had amassed through their
    music industry adventure –
all one million pounds of it –
Discussing this in a cafe in Clerkenwell, Jimmy turned
    to Bill and said:
'I think we should burn it.' –
And they did –
In a boathouse on the island of Jura.

As the author John Higgs – who wrote a whole book
    about
Them – says –
(he's the Keeper of the Queen of Swords) –
'It's one thing to start burning a million pounds –
It's quite another thing to finish burning it' –

Thus Bill and Jimmy still remain the world's greatest
    creators of nothing from something –

They made a pact to not talk about the burning of the
    million quid for 23 years –
and in case any doubt should arise in their minds they
    wrote the contract on the side of a Nissan Bluebird
    and shoved it off Cape Wrath –

Yeah, that'd astound you a Self.

And so last summer 23 years were up –
I met with The Justified Ancients of Mu Mu, aka Bill
and Jimmy, in the same Cafe in Clerkenwell -
Bill told me they were building a pyramid –
They would announce this during a three-day event
marking the 23 year anniversary of the burning of
the million pounds for 400 attendees, all of whom
will be paying volunteers –
In Liverpool –
Would I direct? –
Fuck, Yes –
I made the mistake during that conversation of asking
Bill why they were doing a particular thing –
He looked at me sternly and said:
'As to why, if we knew why, we wouldn't be doing
it' –

Look I could do a whole show just about those three
days –
So if it's of interest, google it up –
Welcome to The Dark Ages will do it –
It damned near killed me, this gig –
But anyway we'll fast forward to the last day of this
epic event –

We're in Toxteth in Liverpool for the Rites of Mu –
The volunteers are painting grotesque skulls on to each
other's faces in readiness for they know not what –
I've managed to get the mic to Jarvis Cocker who is
hidden in a cupboard in a blue hooded robe –
I slip him the Knight of Wands –

He nods as if expecting it –

And the Rites of Mu begin –
Ru and Claire Callender: radical, self-taught
    undertakers from Totnes take to the stage –
They gaze out at a sea of black and white death
    masks –

*'Don't ever be afraid, of anything, ever, because you
 are already dead –*
*This moment, now, this is the moment between the click
 and the bang –*
You are already dead.
*The truth is the glass of life it is not half full, or half
 empty –*
It's smashed on the floor.
And every drop of experience that passes your lips –
is sucked from the teeth of non existence –
We are all absent friends in waiting –
Ancestors already –
peering out through the fabric of our burial shroud –
the soil of our graves filling our mouths –
the flames from our funeral pyres
scorching the inside of our greasy, cracked skulls –
We are already dead.'

The congregation of death masks now openly weep –
They hold each other –
Their black eye make-up running down their white
 painted faces.

'Here's the deal', says Ru.
'MuMufication –
A brick marked with the word Mu –
*A brick that you will hold in your own hands many,
 many times –*

A brick that your children will sneak up to, alone –
in the dark –

to hold silently –
to feel the weight of your oncoming death –
MuMufication –
Then when you die and are burnt –
a portion of your cremated remains are poured into a hole in The Brick –
And The Brick is fired –
And each year on the Toxteth Day of the Dead, The Bricks are ritually cemented together. And so slowly rises The People's Pyramid –
a Pyramid of People –
peaking at 23 feet high –
designed and built using sacred geometry –
A utilitarian, uncompromising statement about mortality and loss –
Ladies and Gentlemen, The Justified Ancients of Mu Mu have entered the funeral business!'

Man – no-one was expecting that –
Talk about a GAP!! –

And after that Jarvis Cocker sings Justifed and Ancient –
And we drag an ice cream van through the streets of Liverpool to a burning pyre –
whilst drummers play traffic cones –
and ragwort is tossed from stolen supermarket trollies –
Why? –
Nobody knows.

And that night, wild eyed and exhausted –
many wounded –
we sit around the fire and marvel:
We're all going to be in a pyramid together –
all of us to be bricks –
stacked and bound together on the Toxteth Day of the
    Dead by the Justified Ancients of Mu Mu –
I mean once you know that, then really, death where is
    thy sting? –

I confided to those gathered around the fire about my
    gastromantical invasion –
One wag suggested that perhaps if my dad had invoked
    Pigspurt by searching for the woman who's arse
    matched his nose –
perhaps I could release myself by finding the man
    whose nose matches my arse?
And feeling emboldened by the activities of the
    previous three days –
pictures are taken of my bare arse in the hair-washing
    pose –
and passed around the fire –
But alas - no matches.

Then a chap arrives at the fire who's been grinning at
    me a lot over the past three days –
'Hello - you remember me?' (he said)
His black and white death mask was smudged all over
    his grinning face –
Oh gosh sorry no, I say –
'You gave me a tarot card in Paris –

I was on the Big Mind course' –
Oh shit right – oh wow –
'You were having a bit of tummy bug this day I think?' –
I changed the subject –
Which card did you get?
'The Fool. Card Zero' –
Ooo. A good one –
'Yes, a very good one.'
I ask, have you come far to be part of this madness? –
'I'm from Geneva' –
Oh! –
'You've been there?' –
Oh no, I've never been there. –
'Oh you spoke as if you had been there.' –
Oh no – I reacted because it's where CERN is –
'Yes, that's where I work' –
You work at CERN? That's extraordinary! –
'Not really. It has 2257 employees' –
You have the CERN grin that my dad talked about! –
'The CERN grin?' –
Yes, he said that everyone at CERN grinned all the time –
'Well', said CERN Grin, 'we do love our work' –
You spend your days wazzing particles together, is that right? –
'Oh I'm not one of the wazzers –
I analyse the wazzer's data –
I am really very low down the pecking order –
The thing that is getting people excited at the moment is the anomalous bottoms' –

Anomalous bottoms? –
'Yes, the bottom mesons are not decaying at the rate they
should be –
Most likely caused by "leptoquarks" or "Z primes" –
but we won't know until we build a larger collider' –
I didn't know what he was talking about either –
I say, you must get asked this all the time –
but is there any chance you're going to set off another Universe inside this one? –
'There's some who would say that that has already happened' –
Seriously?
'But no, I don't think so –
For many of us at CERN, the interest is no longer in the wazzing of particles –
BUT THE NOTHING IN THE TUBE' –
The Nothing?! –
'There is more nothing in CERN than anywhere else in the known universe –
Space is teeming with stuff compared to what they haven't got in CERN' –

You're a Cathar! –
Wait Let me look at your nose.
'Why?'
I want to see if it's an anomalous bottom.
'What?'
If it matches my arse . . .
'Does it?'
Maybe –

And we were round the back of the Ice Kream van–
Indulging in our own protuberential and orificular
　　drama –
Oo, no I wouldn't recommend going down there, I
　　say –
Not after those three days –
But maybe if you're a Cathar –
If you've already accepted that the entire material
　　world is the creation of a mad, barmy, deranged
　　evil demi-urge –
you just get stuck in –
And although it turned out his nose wasn't a perfect
　　match for my arse –
He did give me the CERN grin.

Afterwards back at the fire he opened up about his
　　Catharism –
Why their doctrine was such a threat –
He told me it was their plan to imminentise the
　　eschaton –

You want to bring about the end of the world?! –
(Of course I knew that cos it's the opening line of that
　　book *Illuminatus!*) –

'No' –
He wasn't grinning now –
'This is the mistake everyone makes about us
　　Cathars –
This is why they tried to burn us all –
We don't want to imminentise the eschaton –

We want to immanentise the eschaton!'
Oh, I say – what's the difference?
To imminentise the eschaton is to draw the end of the world nearer –
To *immanantise* the eschaton is the great Cathar goal –
It's to recognise that *the world's end is already here* –
It's inherent and omnipresent! –
We exist on the edge of existence itself! –
This desperate need we all have to know how will the Story end? –
It's a reaction to Gnostic Immanence –
An aversion to the void –
All Story is a conspiracy against Gnostic Immanence –
As a species we're obsessed with protuberential narrative –
Stories that mirror the male orgasm –
Friction, friction, friction, climax, release –
It's very dangerous –
Intolerance for nothing leads to the fantasy of an ending to end all endings –
But we're in the Nothing times now –
The Gap as you like to say –
We're in the midst of collapsing narrative –
Look around –
Don't you see it? –
There's a gap at the centre of every institution –
A lot of sound and fury around the periphery –
But nothing at the centre –
A gap where all the leaders should be –
Where all the experts should be –
A gap in the White House –

A gap at Number 10 –
Even a gap where the Illuminati should be –
I say, and there's a gap where a Self should be too –
'Exactly' says CERN grin –
'Our own divine nothing' –

Back home in Brighton –
I can't leave my bed –
I may have entropy of the bone marrow –
And every time I close my eyes I'm back in MuMu Land –
The Brick Pyramid –
The grotesque black and white faces –

Then Pigspurt wakes me up –
(muffled) *I'm the gap! I'm the gap! –*
What? –
I'm the gap in the brick pyramid in your dream! –
You need to dig me up, get me cremated and put my ashes in a brick! –
Wha – no!
Yes, yes! That's the negation of the negation –
That's psychomagic right there –
This'll be the moment you astound yourself a Self –
This is absurd –
Oh and get the Justified Ancients of Mu Mu to help dig me up! –
Ooo Yes! That'll get us to our climax! –
I might even let you off dog-sledding in Anchorage for this one –

I found I was becoming increasingly powerless to resist the goading –

So, I go and have a meeting with Bill and Jimmy about new plans they're cooking up –
and just before they leave I ask if they'll help me exhume my father –
Bill says, 'wait a minute – you haven't come here to discuss our projects at all –
You've really come so you can ask me and Jimmy if we'll help dig up your dad –
so you can have a good ending for your one-woman-show' –
But I note, they don't say no.

I read up about ancient civilisations who did this sort of thing –
by way of preparing how I might tell my mum –

A few days later I get a phone call from Ru, the Radical self-taught undertaker from Totnes –
Now the keeper of the Death card –

'Daisy – Bill and Jimmy were here discussing the brick practicalities and they told me something that I hope isn't true?' –
What, about digging up Ken?
'Yes! You'll go to jail for a minimum of seven years. It's very very illegal' –
But it does happen? I mean people do get exhumed sometimes don't they?

Contrived, Controlled and Delivered by The Architects to The

THE PEOPLE'S

...TETH DAY OF THE

'Yes, you have to get an exhumation license. If you're
next of kin and you've got a good reason, they
might let you do it –
But I should warn you. It might not be pretty –
What type of soil is he in, do you know?' –
It's a woodland –
'Oh dear. Even after ten years, you can't guarantee that
he's just bones –
It won't be for the faint hearted –
Pigspurt: *To the end of the line, Daisy* –
So I download and print an exhumation license.

It's pages and pages this thing, they don't let you off
lightly –
but I plough through it –
digging out death certificates –
proving I'm me –
Then it finally asked what your reasons are –
And Pigspurt is coming through –
And he writes:
*I recently rectally invoked my father's ghost who
strongly urged me to exhume him, have his remains
cremated and placed into a Mummufication Brick,
also known as a Brick of Mu* –

So I download and print another one and I write:
'Due to changed religious beliefs, I now strongly wish
for my father to be cremated rather than buried' –
John Higgs (Queen of Swords) somehow gets wind of
this plan –
Probably from Ru –

he phones me –
'I have a feeling this is a very bad idea, and that bad
    things may happen if you go ahead –
The word that keeps coming up for me –
and it's odd because it's not a word I ever use –
or even particularly believe in –
is 'immoral' –
My moral need . . .
It's OK, I tell John. It's what you want.
Pigspurt: *That's right. It's what I want. The end of the
    line!* –
*But of course those Undertakers to the Underworld
    only want 23g of my ashes –*
What are you going to do with the rest, Daisy? –
*You could take some of me to Tanna, the island where
    they worship Prince Philip – I must be a bit of a
    god out there too, by now –*
and a bit of me to CERN of course –
and a sprinkle in Montsegur –
Then take the rest to Unst –
Unst? Why? –
WHAT DO WE KNOW ABOUT WHY?
If we knew, we wouldn't be doing it.

My fella Greg shouts –
'I've sent off that form that's been lying about!'
The exhumation form? I shout back –
I'd been procrastinating sending it –
'Yep!' –
But it was still sitting on the pile –
No you haven't! –

"Yes I have!' –
I look at the reasons page –
'Due to changed religious beliefs . . .' –
You've sent the wrong fucking form! You've sent some bureaucrat a form that says I've rectally inhaled his ghost! –
Shit, they'll never let me do it now –
Greg pops his head round the door –
'Your eyebrows are definitely getting longer' –

A few days later, a phone call –
'Oh hello, this is Malcolm Green from Epping Council. We've received your request to exhume your father –
I just have a few questions regarding your reasons –
You say that your father's ghost has been rectally invoked?'
yes –
'And this exhumation is what you wish as next as kin, as well as your father's ghost?' –
I hesitate –
Pigspurt takes over –
Yes Malcolm Green. I want my father to be a brick in the People's Pyramid and be laid to rest by the Justified Ancients of Mu Mu on the Toxteth Day of the Dead –
(It's a terrible impression of me) –
'I see', says Malcolm Green. 'Well, due to the unusual circumstances we have decided to expedite the matter. Your license should be with you by the end of the week' –

I thank him –
'Of course, it's the least I can do –
One can't be too careful with these gastromantical cases'.
I start to make a list of all the people I should tell –
Pigspurt: *The end of the line, Daisy. Very good –
There's a gap - no-one was expecting exhumation comedy –*

I'm put in touch with the Rowland Brothers' Exhumation Services to arrange the details –
The jolly-sounding chap explains the procedure:
There will be a site evaluation and all legal notices will be submitted –
It will take place very early in the morning to ensure privacy –
In summer this will usually mean around 4am –
The site will be screened off –
Health and safety representatives, environmental officers and archaeological supervision will be provided to ensure the deceased is exhumed technically and respectfully –
All human remains and pieces of the original coffin will be placed in the new coffin –
which will then be sealed and identified –
The area of exhumation will be disinfected –
A certificate of clearance will be provided –
My job is to provide evidence that transportation is sorted –
That the crematorium is booked –
And to gather all the necessary letters of permission –

Due to a cancellation they could fit me in in three
    weeks' time –
assuming all the paperwork was in order –
Cost? £6436 + VAT –
Well, says Pigspurt. *What's a Barclaycard for?* –

The next three weeks are a blur of forms –
official phone-calls –
letters of permission –
Horrible, difficult conversations with my family –
But I'm the only next of kin –
So ultimately, as everyone agrees, it is up to me –
But they will not be attending –
Not even the Justified Ancients of Mu Mu can make
    it –
It'll just be me.

And finally, everything is in place –
And it's the night before –
I hardly sleep –
Finally, the alarm rings at 2am –
and I climb in to the car.

I make much better time than I expected –
I'm not due to meet the Rowland Brothers until 4am –
It's still only quarter past three –
I park up and decide to spend some time at the grave
    before the exhumation commences.

It's still dark –
And it's freezing –
I haven't worn enough clothes –

I'd forgotten how cold it is at night –
I look in the boot hoping to find a blanket or some
    clothes in the charity shop boxes –
Nothing –
Except the fat suit.
I think, well, I can wear it til they come –
As soon as I hear them arriving I'll whip it off and
    stash it –
One of the exhumers might give me their jacket –
It's bound to be hot work, exhuming.

So like a crumbling fat babe in the woods –
I make my way to my dad's grave –
Leaving a Hansel and Gretel trail of pink foam crumbs behind me.
At the grave I sit down amongst the pine cones and fallen leaves –
And look at the wooden grave marker with the gap where Dad's face should be.

So this will be the end of the line, right Dad? –
This has got to be the negation of the negation? –
Pigspurt has gone strangely quiet –

Then I see it –
A morel mushroom –
WTF? –
A morel –
My morel need! –
And I'm picturing all the shocked faces as I told people what I was doing –
My mum –
My kids –
All those concerned phone calls –
People genuinely worried about me –
My moral need!
I have to make this madness stop –
What I'm doing is just intolerance of the void –
I need to face the gap –
Stop this protuberential narrative to the end of the line that Pigspurt has cooked up –

Pigspurt awakes –
Think you can get rid of me that easily? –
Invoke a bit of Nothing-Worship and I'll be on my way? –
There is nothing, absolutely nothing, that should stand in the way of a good story –
And I don't mean the fake stories that don't happen in life –
I mean the real shit –
And if that means burning a million pounds, then that's what you've got to do –
If it means digging up your dead dad –
Well if you've had the idea it's too late! –
No! It's not too late –
It's a false climax! –
It's no good thinking I can just dig up my dad and turn him into a brick and job done –
end of the line reached –
negation of the negation achieved –
nothing is ever as simple as that!
The problem with the end of the world is that it doesn't end! –
The show must go on –
There'll just be another end of another line –
Pigspurt: *Then we'll find the negation of the negation of the negation! –*
You made a deal, girl –
And you've already told my tales as if they were yours –
But please –
I don't want to dig you up –

I really don't want to –
What did you expect it to be like at the end of the line? –
This is just like you –
to give up your chance to astound yourself a self –
To do something of NOTE! –

Do something of note?! –
Do something of note?!
I was stuck up your arsehole all my life –
and I managed to turn the tables and got you stuck up mine –
That was something of note! –

But it's time now, Dad –
It's time for me to make peace with The Gap.
Ha! I'm not your Dad! Your dad's dead –
buried ten years ago here in Epping Forest –
His story is long since over –
Who are you then?
I'M THE MAD BARMY DERANGED EVIL
   DEMIURGE –
PIGSPURT! –
I'M THE ONE WHO'S JOB IT IS TO GOAD YOU
   FUCKERS TO THE END OF THE LINE –
TO IMMINENTISE THE ESCHATON –
EVERYONE WANTS TO KNOW HOW IT'S GOING
   TO END? –
WITH A WHIMPER OR A BANG? –
AND I'M THE ONE WHO'LL SHOW YOU –
DIG UP YOUR DADDY DAISY! –
YOU MADE A PACT WITH PIGSPURT

And I'm pulling chunks of the crumbling fat suit away
   from me –
and I'm screaming –
Look at me! –
Look at me exactly as I am! –
I am not an unsuccessful man! –
I am a woman! –
And then not just the fat suit is coming off –
but all my clothes –

But Pigspurt has full control of my body now –
And he's digging –

With my bare hands –
There's strange demon-pig sounds emanating from my
    stomach –

It takes all my power to stop my hands from digging –
Then I get it! –
I KNOW WHO YOU ARE! –
You're not the mad barmy deranged evil demiurge –
You're not even Pigspurt –
You're my Storyteller! –
I've been tricked! By my own storyteller –
I so over-fed you with set-ups –
Now you've found the only possible way to pay
    everything off –

So Pigspurt is just the first little geezer inside my
    Storyteller –
If I can just find the little geezer who's inside
    Pigspurt –
and then the little geezer who's inside that one –
and the other tiny geezer who's inside that one –
and the tinier geezer –
and the tinier geezer –
and the tinier –
and the tinier –
and the tinier –
and the tinier –
and the tinier –

And finally I find it –
I force open A GAP –
It's a note! –
Done anything of note?
A NOTE is a single unit of NOTHING! –
The Archon Domain of Eternal Incredible Laughter! –
I've found the orificular end of the line! –
The true negation of the negation –

I'm dimly aware of torchlight approaching now
    through the dusky trees –

And I know my next step –
I can see a whole new form of bollocks! –
Psychomagical bollocks –
I'll call in the keepers of the cards –
We'll re-open The Tilly Matthew Academy of Bizarre
    and Adventurous Education -
And together we will oversee a breakthrough at
    CERN! –
Usher in the Gnothing!
Welcome the Collapsing Narrative –
Let the light and laughter in through the Gaps! –
And unlearn everything! –

'Daddy's Dreams!' shouts Pigspurt.
The remains of the fat suit dangle around my naked
    body –
The exhumation team arrive –
Just as my Bamsie Strings finally give way –
Oh God – oh Christ –

It's a Beef Tea Blowback –

Now that's what I call Catharsis.

As they escort me away from the grave –
I look up at Mr Rowland, the chief exhumer –
I say, you know - your nose looks exactly like my
    arse . . .

(Yes, that's the third act climax – now we've just got
    the resolution bit)

Plans are coming along for the pilgrimage to CERN –
So if you'd like to join me and a few other
Cathars –
Money Burners –
Discordians –
For Psychomagical Bollocks with the God of
    Gnothing –
well, you'd be very welcome.
(drop me an email daisy@the-mycelium.com)

Don't forget to sign up for MuMufication –
at www.MuMufication.com –
The first ever Toxteth Day of the Dead will be on
    November 23rd 2018 –
when the first bricks will be laid –
Hopefully not yours –
although some of you look a bit dicky.

The exhumation didn't go ahead –
Mr Rowland couldn't in all good faith tick the box that

    said I was sound of mind –
But he is an extraordinary man –
And Christ, we had a good laugh that morning –
Let in the Archon Domain of Eternal Incredible
    Laughter for sure –
He's coming to CERN –
We'll definitely need an exhumer –

Did Pigspurt ever return? –
No –
I've not attempted the old gastromancy again –
too dangerous –
and not great for the digestion –
But that wasn't Ken –
And now that I am purged of Pigspurt –
my actual dad comes better into view –

Because he wasn't just the goader –
the antic visionary –
the genius in the original sense of the word –
He was also just my dad.
My generous, sentimental, inspiring, warm and funny
    dad –

So gastromantical invocation, not so much –
But moments when he comes into my mind, focused
    and clear –

Like this one:

'Well done, kiddo. Pretty well structured, I thought –
Got most of your set-ups paid off –

Rather good the way you made the antagonist narrative
   itself –
It was a thing of note.'
Thanks Dad –
'You'll astound yourself your own Self eventually –
Of that much I'm sure –
No good walking around with a Self not of your own
   astounding, is it?'
No. But I made some of it up, Dad –
'Yeah – no pies for us, Daisy. No pies' –
I said, you know you've left this gap, this nothing,
   where my dad should be –
And it's not the Cathar's jolly nothing –
Maybe I should see if Pigspurt could infest me again?
Dad: 'Listen to me! –
It's all you, you fool –
Just cos you put on a ridiculous nasal voice when you
   say mad things doesn't mean it hasn't come from
   you –
Pigspurt is in you and always will be –
It was your own nose you sought.

Onward girl –
The Archon Domain of Eternal Incredible Laughter
   won't let itself in through the gaps, you know' –
OK Dad –

All societies tremble –
when the scornful aristocracy of the tramps –
the inaccessibles –
the rulers over the ideal –
and the conquerors of nothing –
resolutely advance –
So come on iconoclasts, forward –
Already the foreboding sky –
Grows dark and silent –
For we are full of sound and fury –
Signifying Gnothing . . .

Review of Pigspurt's Daughter

by Jason Watkins

Jason Watkins' review of *Pigspurt's Daughter* won the Observer/Anthony Burgess Prize for Arts Journalism 2019. Jason Watkins is a special needs teacher and tutor for pupils out of education based in Otley, West Yorkshire. He previously worked in TV and as a film researcher.

In naming his daughter after the Greek goddess of discord and misrule, maverick director/actor/playwright Ken Campbell gave her a lot to live up to. *Pigspurt's Daughter*, a solo show by Daisy Eris Campbell to mark the 10th anniversary of her father's death, is a window on a remarkable parent-child relationship bound by a love of logic-defying overstimulation and an aversion to anything routine or everyday.

"Loomed large" is the key epithet for Ken Campbell's life and work, and when meeting his adult daughter his opening gambit would often be: "Done anything of note lately?" A celebrated provocateur, his legendary stage productions included 22-hour plays and pidgin English versions of Shakespeare. Campbell cut an imposing, eccentric figure, someone who would literally wear his obsessions on his sleeve. This is brought to life when, amid the clutter of her father's career, Daisy Campbell dons his iconic fishing jacket, which doubled as his "office". Pigspurt's Daughter is about moving out of the shadow of a daunting, challenging genius while retaining a deep, abiding love for him.

Rather than sombre memorial, the play grapples with loss via a welter of fringe and countercultural topics. Among other things, it takes in particle physics, neurology, the Cathars, divination, self-discovery workshops and the end of the world, which on paper sounds like being cornered by a foaming-at-the-mouth conspiracy theorist. However, Daisy Campbell manages to channel the poetic flow of the rant and the tirade into a piece of storytelling that is absurdist high drama and a moving chronicle of living in the orbit of goading, demanding brilliance.

What emerges is that Ken Campbell bequeathed an ethos of belligerent anti-mindfulness to his daughter, instilling a love of heady, outlier views and philosophies. For both, life and art is about bombarding the mind and relishing the connections and coincidences that materialise. In a play overloaded with themes, a key motif emerges: what happens to the self when you devote your life to the anarchic and the arcane? Pigspurt's Daughter reveals the psychic toll of the quest for ideas that confound rather than confirm expectations.

Campbell talks of being sectioned wearing rainbow-coloured knickers on her head and being pronoid (the opposite of paranoia – everyone is conspiring to help you). She describes her exhaustion after working with the KLF, the band that burned a million pounds. Campbell organised the band's darkly carnivalesque 2017 comeback. Asking the reasons behind their freewheeling demands, she was told: "If we knew why, we wouldn't do it" – an uncompromising, gnomic approach that chimes with her father's directorial style. He would tell his actors: "I will give you impossible things to do then shout at you when you can't do them." This metaphysical unruliness is the territory of a loosely aligned group of rebel thinkers and seekers drawn to the wellspring of discordianism (a shifting ground of conspiracy theory and trickster doublespeak designed to enlighten through bewilderment; a Zen politics that undercuts bedrock ideologies, granting glimpses of "the real truth"). Pigspurt's Daughter is in part a valediction to the conceptual excess of discordianism, of losing oneself in a headlong rush of tumultuous notions and beliefs, and becomes a tale of finding structure, meaning and emotional truth.

As the play unfolds, it becomes clear that storytelling itself is central to Campbell's relationship with both her father and the world at large. When she was 11, her father took her to an intense three-day seminar on story structure by screenwriting guru Robert McKee. McKee's models and jargon percolate through the whole of Pigspurt's Daughter. Setups, payoffs, negation of a payoff (or twist) and the "negation of the negation" all recur and shape the narrative, creating an underpinning compositional knowingness that belies the play's rambling, digressive feel.

Pigspurt's Daughter deals with the loss of a towering individual. Nina Conti, protege and lover of Ken Campbell, went through a similar exorcism with her touching film Her Master's Voice, and Daisy Campbell finds suitably outre metaphors for her father's stature and her personal loss. At one point she is trapped, crushed and buried under the mass of material in her father's archive. She bows out with a tall tale about gaining a licence to disinter her father, becoming increasingly hysterical (in every sense) as her plan comes together.

In Pigspurt's Daughter, spurning reality looks like gruelling fun. In truth, discordianism has become less enticing in an age of global chaos and disinformation. Yet, while boisterously cartwheeling through a dense array of peripheral, underground subjects, Daisy Campbell succeeds in conveying many things – remembrance and self-assertion, fantasy and confession, grief and joy. The play imparts a very personal message: never revel in the ordinary, cherish those near and dear to us, and don't go (too) mad.

Some Family Photos

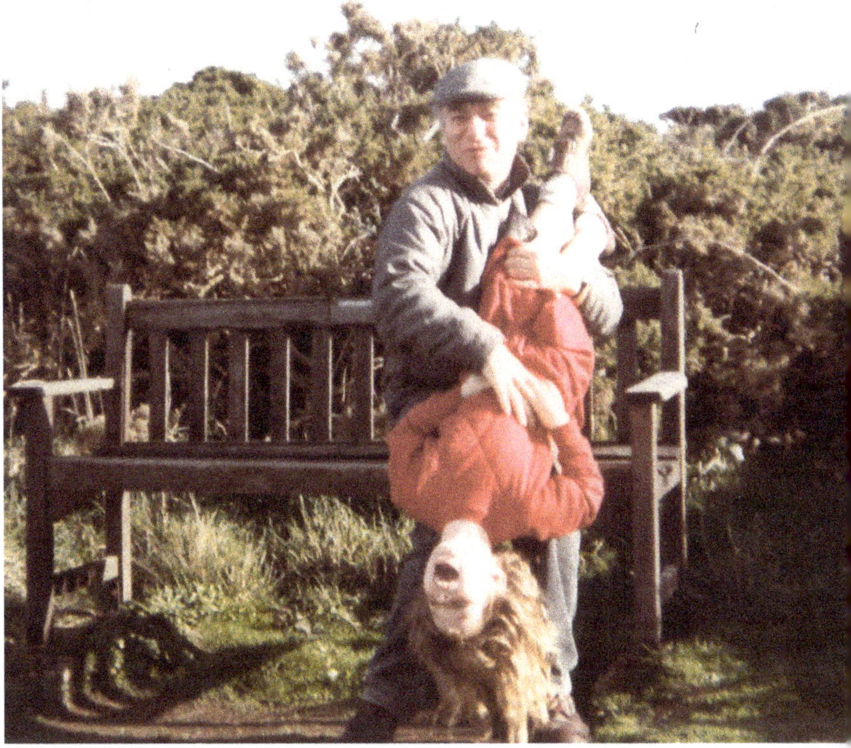

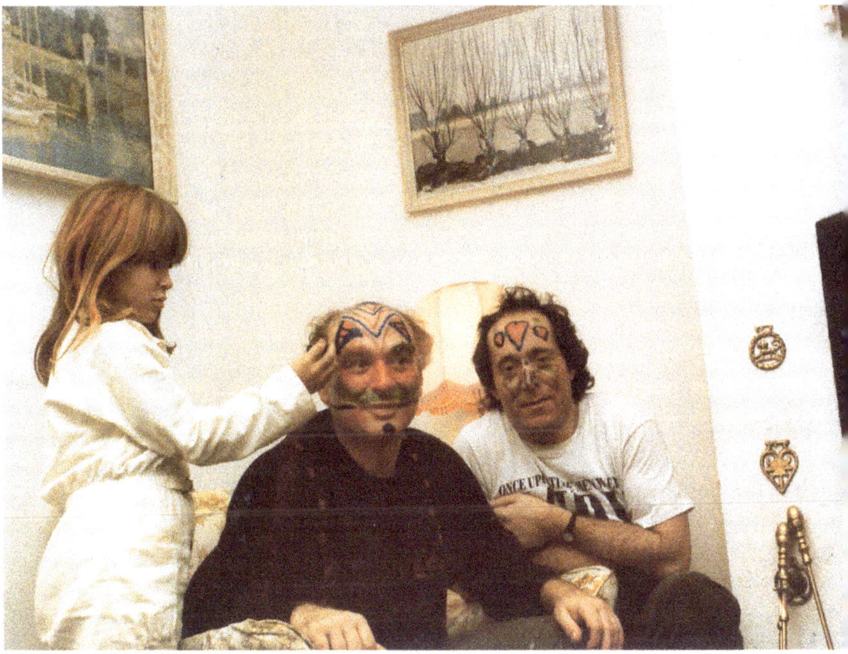

Publishing the Books of Robert Anton Wilson
and Other Adventurous Thinkers

hilaritaspress.com

www.ingramcontent.com/pod-product-compliance
Lightning Source LLC
Chambersburg PA
CBHW051549010526
44118CB00022B/2637